# KINDLE PUBLISHING FOR ENTREPRENEURS

### 9 STEPS TO PRODUCING BEST SELLING AMAZON KINDLE BOOKS AND BUILDING INCREDIBLE PASSIVE INCOME

## ENTREPRENEUR PUBLISHING

# COPYRIGHT

# DISCLAIMER

# FREE GIFT

# Kindle 5 Star Books

## Free Kindle 5 Star Book Club Membership

Join Other Kindle 5 Star Members Who Are Getting Private Access To Weekly Free Kindle Book Promotions

### Get free Kindle books

Stay connected:

Join our Facebook group

Follow Kindle 5 Star on Twitter

Also, if you want to receive updates on Entrepreneur Publishing's new books, free promotions and Kindle countdown deals sign up to their New Release Mailing List.

For entrepreneurs: http://www.entrepreneurfinesse.com

# TABLE OF CONTENTS

# INTRODUCTION

Kindle Publishing for Entrepreneurs contains proven steps that will help you write an eBook that when published can help bring notoriety and makes you more passive income all in good time. This eBook will teach you how to make great books for readers who will be visiting the Amazon Kindle platform.

This book will also teach you how to come up with your own great eBook by giving you tips on what and how to write. This is also inclusive of editing and preparation of a great cover image that looks awesome and sends the right message. You will also learn how to upload this image without corrupting the quality.

Publishing your kindle eBook on Amazon is not a hard process but there are tips that you can use to ensure that you do it properly. Publishing is all about coming up with content that your target audience relates to and will be willing to purchase.

Thanks again for downloading this book, I hope you enjoy it!

# CHAPTER 1: DEFINING YOUR AUDIENCE

It is very important to be clear about your target audience, i.e: the individual or group you wish to sell your product to. The book you write must then be written keeping your target audience in mind so that they are interested in buying it and can also enjoy its benefits.

When writing an eBook you should have some ideas on how to attract your audience. Online readers are not very patient people when it comes to looking for something and they only stop to read something that looks attractive to them, and it is evident that you can't have sales if no one reads your eBook. To make your job interesting and to attract the right target audience is not that hard of a task, you just need to know the right buttons to push. You should be able to define your target audience by the points explained below.

## Demography

This is focused on the socioeconomic characteristics of people in a given region. When it comes to profiling the audience that you plan on offering your products to, you should ensure that they are interested in what you have to offer and they would be willing to pay for it. Demographic information will guide you well in this endeavor and can even give you ideas of another business after studying the people in a certain region and realizing that they can consume some other product too. Here are some demographic factors that you should put into consideration while looking for an audience:

- Age
  You must be well aware of your target audience's age. For example, if you are targeting children then you will have to use simple vocabulary and avoid erotic stuff. On the other hand, if you are writing for teens then you should have things that they are interested in such as romance and fantasy.

- Gender
  There are things that women love to read about that men don't and vice versa. So when you are looking for the right target audience, first decide which gender you wish to target. However, there are some topics that are well in demand by both men and women.

- Occupation
  You can tell a lot about someone by the type of job they do. If you have some high pro-file job, chances are, you're a sophisticated person, and hence you will be interested in specific topics. There are several eBook ideas based about certain occupations, such as tips etc. hence this point is of importance.

- Education

Literate and illiterate people have a slightly different taste in many things, for example when it comes to reading, the illiterate cannot buy books which they cannot read. For you to be selling an eBook means that the audience that you target should be literate.

- Marital Status
  This is very important because your topic selection largely depends on your target audience's marital status. For example, if they are married you can write content related to husband-wife issues, bringing up a child etc.

- Income Level
  This will give you a very good idea on who to sell to, what to sell and at what price. People who earn a lot of money tend to spend on lavish items and can afford to pay more. Finding a target market of high income people and finding some of the commodities that they are much interested in will see you make some decent sales.

- Average Family Size
  If you are looking to be selling eBooks and your target audience is made up of huge families, it would make sense to sell books that are relevant to kids so that the parents can purchase some for their kids. With the right products, large families can be really great markets for one to invest in.

All this information will help you come up with custom content that is fit for the audience that you just profiled. At times you might find that within one big geographical area, there is more than one profile of people and this can be a great idea for you to invest in. But understand that demographics are just one part of the solution, you need to pay attention to several other things.

## Address The Consumers Questions

A consumer who goes online to look for products that they want to buy often gets confused and ends up having numerous questions. There are a great number of online retailers and hence the buyer often gets confused about the selection of a store. It is your work as a retailer to ensure that you address these questions and give comprehensive answers so that the consumer can trust and want to buy from you by picking you over other alternatives.

When dealing with people especially on social network platforms you should use content of high quality. Answer their questions and then help the consumer solve whatever issue they might be facing. Good and informative solutions will lead to them sharing your solutions to their friends and this will create a much bigger fan base for you and that results in more potential clients. Writing and publishing eBooks that help common people solve their day to day issues could be a huge hit with a large customer base.

## Understand The Potential Consumer

When profiling a group of people that you have the hopes of making your clients, you should first understand them better. This has been made easier today by the use of social media networks; you can learn a lot about someone even without talking to them. You can learn someone's favorite things, places that they like to visit social media platform that they like using and the ways that they prefer when gathering information. Look to understand what the customer cares about for; if you are able to show that you understand and share their concern, you will be able to create a long-term relationship that will be beneficial to the both of you.

# CHAPTER 2: YOUR OWN SELF-PUBLISHING PLATFORM OF CHOICE

After you have established your target audience, it is time to move to the next step. You should strive on making sure that the channel that you will use to get your products to your customers is not shady and that it works well for them. One thing you should know about sales is that the customer is always right –whatever the customer wants should be provided.

As a writer you are obliged to answer your audience's questions and listen to their feedback so that you can be able to forge an audience base that is big and that will withstand the test of time.

When it comes to publishing platforms you have several choices including Amazon Kindle Direct Publishing, and even your own blog. While publishing and selling the eBook on your own blog and finding an online payment platform of your liking may prove to give you more income per eBook but with a lot of marketing. At the end of the day you want a platform that will give you time to focus on other things like coming up with more books.

Other than a higher percentage income per eBook, the other benefit of using your own blog is that you can even elaborate on some parts of your book that your readers might have problems in. You can even borrow topics from the book and expound on them in the blog.

You will also get direct feedback since buyers on Amazon since buyers are on the site looking for things to buy anyway. You can read the feedback and improve in your next book. Feedback also boosts your morale if it is positive and if negative, it motivates you to improve so as to have better sales in your next book.

When you use your blog as a publishing platform you also have the chance of increasing you fan base which means that you will be able to sell more and more if you could match the quality and expectations. You can also network with people who think like you on your blog; networking is very important when you are dealing with online work. These groups of likeminded people exchanging ideas can lead you to coming up with a masterpiece.

## Understanding How Amazon Kindle Publishing Works

If you have written a book and are looking at how you can have it published and sold on Amazon then the solution is right here.

You need to go online and open an account on Kindle Direct Publishing. If you happen to have an Amazon account, you can just use the login information to log in to the Kindle publishing site.

If you are an American you will be required to produce you social security number for taxation as it is a requirement by the federal government. You also need to enter your payment information on how you will be receiving your money once your eBook starts to make sales. It is wise to enter your bank information as soon as possible otherwise the royalties from your books will be sent to you in the form of checks in the currency of the marketplace where your books were sold. This takes longer to get to you and the amount of money that reaches you after the deductions and conversion of the currency is not that desirable. The taxation process can be a little tricky depending on what country you are from and how you do business, it would be wise if you were to contact a legal advisor to help you sort it out.

## Description Writing Guidelines

When you are writing your book description ensure that you give a nice summary of all that is contained in the book in a few words. You should avoid the use of pornographic and offensive content in your book for they can be read by anyone. Make sure that there are no advertisements in the description, watermarks on images, information that is time sensitive, reviews or testimonials, phone numbers and other contact information, also ensure that you do not give prices and alternative venues of purchasing the book. Soliciting readers for positive reviews is prohibited too.

## Publishing and Unpublishing Flexibility

You should also know that you can easily unpublish your books with very few steps. The good thing about this option is that if you find your book to have some issues that need altering, you can just unpublish it and correct the problem, then republish it. You just go to bookshelf in your account and select the "unpublish" box and tick on it and your book is unpublished and will become unavailable to buyers in less than seventy-two hours. Once you are through with your corrections and are ready to put it back up, it will take you about twelve-hours to republish. But if you are just looking to alter some minor changes, you could just edit the book while it is still on sale by going to your bookshelf and selecting the button for editing. After you are finished, just select to republish.

## Recommended Formats

The preferred formats for you eBook on Kindle Direct Publishing include any one of the following:

- Microsoft Word
- Mobi
- HTML and
- Zipped HTML files

These formats enable your customers to be able to open and read the eBooks once they buy them. For formatting such as bold, italics or headers in your work, you can do that in the source document before you start formatting it for publication.

## Cost and Digital Rights

When publishing your eBook on Kindle store you will not be charged if you are using the Kindle Direct Publishing but you must have digital rights. Digital rights are what allow one to access, use, create and even publish digital media in relation to protection of privacy and freedom of expression. The application of digital rights management helps protect your work and prevent people from copying it, once activated it cannot be undone. If you had books written before it was available you can add it to your older titles and enjoy the protection.

## Getting an Updated Copy

If you had purchased a book and it happens to be updated by the writer, you can contact the Kindle store and enjoy the updated copy at no extra cost. The store has not yet come up with a way of getting the updated book; you have to contact them directly, though there should be one very soon.

The points provided above are there to help you understand the publishing process and once you understand that, you will have an easier time when it comes to publishing. Saving time when publishing and dealing with sales creates more free time for you and this will enable you to come up with more quality eBooks.

## Benefits of Using Kindle Direct Publishing (KDP)

There are numerous platforms that you can use for the publishing of an eBook, your blog included. The thing about using KDP is that it has some benefits that you will not find somewhere else. Some of them include the following:

- High Royalties Awarded

  Signing up with Kindle Direct Publishing Select puts your eBook into the kindle library where you earn a certain percentage of money when an online visitor reads over ten percent of your book. You can also earn a percentage when someone logs in to the library and lends your book.

When someone from Japan, Mexico, Brazil or India buys your book on KDP select, you will make a seventy percent royalty.

- Maximize The Potential of Book Sales

  You have two promotional kits to choose from when on Kindle. You can either go with the Kindle Countdown Deals, which earns you royalties as a discount promotional for your book and is time-bound; or use the Free Book Promotion tool, in which your book is available free for a limited duration all around the world.

- Large Audience

  When using your blog as a place to market your eBook, you only have a limited number of followers who can buy it from you. On the other hand, if you decide to work with Amazon Kindle Direct Publishing Select, you will have a very wide market in an instant. Markets such as Japan, Mexico, the U.S and Germany are great places to be selling in.

# CHAPTER 3: WRITING THE BOOK

When you plan on writing an eBook, the very first thing that you should do is come up with an idea on which you will base your book. When you come up with the idea, make sure that there is a market for that kind of book. You are writing to make money and not for fun. Though it is better if you choose a title that you are more familiar with, this will make you do a little or no research at all and that saves you a lot of time.

When you are writing on a topic that you are familiar with you tend to enjoy writing. If you are happy about what you are writing, there are very high chances that you will see the project thoroughly. If you choose a topic just because you think it will make you more money, the long researches may bore you enough for you to quit.

## Planning

After coming up with a great and lucrative idea you should come up with a plan that you will follow in writing the eBook. You can use your mind maps to plan for; they help you see the connection between ideas, follow through and creation of an outline. Make an outline that you think could help you benefit from the topic if you did not know anything about it.

## Writing

When you start to write it is wise to start with an outline followed by an introduction and then move on to the first paragraph. One way of simplifying your writing could be by dividing the chapters of the book each into a blog of its own. When you are through with the blogs you will then edit them together into one big document. The positive thing about this style of writing is that you can start with sections that you are very good at rather than being stuck at the beginning. With half of the book done, you will have the motivation to complete the other half. Use Microsoft Word to write your books as it is simple to use and it can be converted into any other format.

## Creating A Template

The next thing you need to do is to come up with a template in which you will be writing your book. Choose the correct page size that can be readable in most computer screens. Then select the font type that you will be using for you titles, chapters, subtitles and the main content. Select a font type that one can read more than fifty pages of, without hurting his or her eyes. Finally select the sizes of the fonts that you will be using for the different things you will be writing. You can use graphics and logos but do not overdo it unless the graphics are showing something very relevant to the information you are providing.

After making the template with all the subtopics, you are now ready to immerse yourself into the writing. Make sure that the tone you use is in sync with the message that you are trying to convey.

## THINGS THAT SHOULD BE FOUND IN A COMPLETE EBOOK

### Disclaimer Page Copyrighting

A disclaimer helps protect the writer in case someone decides to sue you for some reason known to him. It states that what you have written is your own opinion on the topic and not a guide of some sort. It also states that you are not guaranteeing something and people who read the book should use their conclusions and not what the book suggests.

The copyright is there to help you by protecting your work such that no one else can reproduce the same. If someone steals your work for whatever reason you are allowed to take them to court and press charges.

### Great eBook Cover

It is said that first impressions last long, this is very true even when it comes to selling and buying of products. As the owner of the product, you do your best to ensure that the packaging of your goods is looking good and attractive to the consumers. The consumer will first see the cover of the eBook before anything else, you can use Photoshop to edit a nice cover or hire someone to do it for you if you have no Photoshop knowledge, though it is super easy to learn.

### A Preface

If you want to gain some credibility with your readers, start by letting them know about your intentions for writing the book. A short story or history of the eBook can be very helpful to the readers; it will help them understand the message in the book better.

### A Page about the Author

This helps you as the writer to get a little personal with your audience and readers. It is normally found at the end of the book but you can place at the front to have the readers learn about you to build up the excitement of your work.

### Contacts

When you come to the very end of your book you can include some ways that the readers can get in touch with you if they have any questions or feedback.

## Links

Links are very great tools for they help you when you are trying to get a point across. By sending someone to the page where the query they might have is well explained and elaborated helps them a lot. You can also use them to link to your account so that the reader can get more information on your webpage. If you are looking to linking to a third party's webpage, ensure that they are okay with it first.

## Exercises, Helpful Tools and Calculators

It is smart to put some helpful tools relevant to the topics that your eBook will be covering. You can also add some questions based on what is in the book, for the reader to see if they understood the book once they are done.
Adding of these tools will help in making your eBook very helpful and look more professional too.

You can use the tools as a marketing stunt, say that you have given the tools in the book for free, this makes you seem generous and trustworthy.

## Time Taken To Complete

The time that it will take you depends entirely on you and your writing speed and the schedule that you are working on. Writing does not take a long time really, just set aside a few hours a day and work on it. Find a peaceful place to be working at, somewhere where no one will come to interrupt you as you do your thing.
Let whoever you live with know that you are busy and lock yourself in your room and work.

Once you are through with writing the book, set it aside for sometime before going through if for editing. The reason for the short break is so that you get to see it with a fresh perspective. Make sure that you do not edit your book as you write it, you might be tired and repeat a mistake even after editing it again.

Check for any information that you might have talked about more than once in the book in a similar way. Ensure that there is no missing information that you might have left out while writing. Also check to see if the flow of chapters is great as is or should be tweaked a little bit. Correct all these mistakes and ensure that the book looks great.

Read through and correct silly typos and confusing sentences. Check for misspellings and words that might be omitted while writing.

# Chapter 4: Formatting

Once you are through with writing the eBook, the next thing to do is to format it in a specific way that is suitable for your target audience and the platform that you are going to be distributing it through. There are more than fifty formats that you can convert your word document into. As stated before, you choose a format based on the outlet platform of your choice. Here are some of the most common formats and the platforms that they are best compatible with:

## Word Format

When publishing with Kindle Direct Publishing it accepts most DOC and DOCX files for conversion. However, files that contain formatting that is too complex may not be converted well. After you have converted you files, go through them to see whether they have converted properly.

Font, page numbers and margins that had been set in Word do not apply on Kindle; eBooks are available in different sizes as the customer wants. Images that are to be added in the eBook should be added to the document by being inserted and not by copy pasting.

When sending your work in this format, make sure that the whole book is in one large file and not in separate ones. When you submit them separately, the KDP will read and embed the image of your products as the cover page of the eBook.

## MOBI

The only MOBI format that is supported is the .mobi format that is created using Amazon tools that are supported and recommended such as KindleGen.

## HTML

Kindle Direct Publishing only accepts the files in HTML format if they are zipped before being uploaded. None of the other file formats can upload while zipped. When saving your html file, use web page or filtered HTML and HTM if you are using your PC: or Web page .html if you are using a Mac., this includes even the images, then zip the files and upload them.

## Plain Text

This format is great for files that have no images because when converted to HTML, TXT files lose their images and cannot display them.

## EPUB

It is imperative that you validate your ePUB file using Kindler Previewer or Kindler Gen to ensure that the file is converted properly. Kindle Direct Publishing is able to convert ePUB files while they are still unzipped.

Kindle Package Format and Rich Text Format

These two can be converted by the Kindle Direct Publisher into files that can be used by the writer.

## PDF

Portable Document Format is a file system that was developed by Adobe Systems and it has the ability to capture information from numerous publishing applications on your desktop. This flexibility makes it a preferred format for transferring documents for you can have them however you want them. You can only read files in this format by the use of an Adobe Reader. Adobe Reader is a free application that is compatible with any computer and once installed you will only be clicking on the file you want to read and the application will just start up. This is why PDF is one of the most heavily used formatting methods.

Some Things You Can Do With A PDF

- You can make the bookmark area hierarchical to make some drop down menus, which are easy-to-navigate.
- It gives you the option of setting your eBook to always open the first page and in the best possible size.
- A navigation sidebar that lets you jump to wherever you want to in the eBook is a nice trick that will help you read the book thoroughly.
- Creating of forms and embedded tools is a possibility and helps in making your reading easier.

Converting the word document is not very difficult, just click the save button and choose the "save as PDF" option. Make sure that you have edited and proofread the Word Document before converting it, for it is easier to edit it while it is a Word Document rather than a PDF file.

After you have converted the document, sync the page numbers, put the print icons and add up all the navigation things and bookmarks. Once you have finished doing all these, save the file.

## PDF SECURITY

It is not possible to guarantee complete security while dealing with Adobe PDF because people can steal the information on your document very easily. Do not be disappointed that your work will all be stolen; there is quite a good number of honest people out there.

Adobe has some precautions that you can take to protect your work. They might not be super effective but when used properly they can reduce the risk. You can create a password in order to monitor the people who have access to the page, however this pisses off the paying customers and that makes it customer unfriendly.

You can instead set the document such that it cannot be copied, changed or edited. You should only make the document able to be copied if the information you are offering will need the consumer to make some printouts.

You can also try to get the consumer not to share the eBook with their friends by trying to explain how hard you had to work on the book. Tell them how much you would appreciate if they did not give away those free copies. This method works from time to time depending on who buys your eBook.

Your book is now ready to hit the market and all you need is to make it available it to your online consumers.

# CHAPTER 5: KINDLE QUALITY CONTENT GUIDE

Customers who shop on Amazon expect very high standards when it comes to services and products sold there. Kindle Direct Publishing sells on Amazon and therefore it has to produce eBooks that are of high quality with no mistakes at all. If the customer finds a mistake and they alert Amazon, then the Amazon staff reaches out to the writer asking to correct the issue quickly and also provide some options on how to avoid making the same mistake again.

This chapter is going to focus on helping you to properly understand these minor and silly mistakes, to prepare you for them so that when you are writing you do not make such mistakes. Pay attention to these errors and avoid them when working on your project.

When it comes to reviewing your book, it is highly recommended that you do it using the Kindle Previewer. This app helps you see exactly how you work will look like on different Kindle apps and devices.

## ERRORS

After you are done writing your book, it is imperative that you go through it one or two times looking for errors before uploading the file. Errors that can be made are different and they vary in severity and the damages that they might cause. Critical issues are errors that can cause the book to be incomplete or unusable. Since they considerably affect the reader's experience, they result in the book being dropped from sales till all corrections are taken care of.

### The Errors Found On a Document

#### Unsupported Characters

When you use characters that are not supported on kindle, they will appear as funny boxes and strings of characters you do not understand when you take your text to the Previewer software. Run your entire book through the Previewer to review it for any unwanted characters to ensure that your customers have only the best products.

#### Fixing Unsupported Characters

When reviewing your book, if you happen to come across a word with unsupported characters, use the Kindle Previewer to check for the same word in the whole document to correct it. One unsupported character indicates that there might be many more in the document so be keen while reviewing a book. To be on the safe side go through the Kindle Publishing Guidelines and find out which characters are not supported and which are.

## Typos

When writing an eBook, make sure that you do not have any typos. They are minor but common mistakes that people make. You can easily cause them due to a lack of attention, poor scanned character recognition, poorly copy pasting etc. Typos are the highest reported errors in writing and for you to write a great book, ensure that you avoid them completely.

Examples of typos can include replacing numbers with letters and vice versa, poor punctuation of words, junk characters, use of soft hyphens, missing letters in your words and use of HTML tags in places where you should use characters. At times a simple typo can change the meaning of an entire sentence.

For example: A steel pan and a steel pen, are two completely different things and a simple mistake can ruin the meaning making it difficult for the reader interpret what is being said.

## Prevention and Fixing of Typos

Use the tools provided, such as the Kindler Previewer to search for any mistakes in your eBook. It also assists you in locating multiple typo problems and corrects them.
Sometime an author can use dialects spellings intentionally in his work, this are not considered as errors. If you find a word that you have made a typo in, check the whole document for that word, chances are you might have repeated the mistake multiple times in the document.

## The Cover

When you are editing your book's cover design make sure that you make it as high quality and precise as possible. If the cover image impresses the reader, chances are they will buy the book. To ensure that your cover image is the best, avoid:

- Using an image that is too big or small that when the book is being viewed, it does not display the full image or it shows a small image with white margins.
- Using an image that is of poor quality, i.e: that it appears blurry when displayed on the screen.
- Inserting the cover image into the Word file, this will cause an error.
- Forgetting to use the cover image in the first place.

You can easily correct some of these mistakes by just being attentive. Keep a reminder of things to do to your book before viewing it on Kindle Previewer. You can also learn how to size up and convert images so that they maintain their quality. Most cover images start up as high quality images and turn into low quality images when you start converting them into formats that are friendly to the platform you want to use.

Some of the solutions for correcting your image include the following:

### Image Quality

When it comes to images, you want them to be clear and helpful to the reader in understanding the information on that page. Readers tend to respond well to books with images that elaborate further on the information provided in the page. You should review your eBook on Kindle Previewer to ensure that the images and the text are all clear and readable. To make sure that your readers don't get annoyed by how your book is portrayed, ensure that everything is in its place as needed.

Using scanned images is not advisable as they make the book look bad. If your eBook has such images, the Kindle store might not sell them as they are unreadable on the kindle device and it is also impossible for the readers to change the text size. However, in certain cases this rule may be exempted, especially where the images do not have text or explanation.

### How To Ensure High-Quality Images

The best and simplest way of ensuring that the images in your books are of high quality is by making sure that when importing images you use the ones with the highest quality possible.

### Ensuring Correct Formatting

Formatting problems are those that appear on the surface of the pages involving things such as excess spacing in between paragraphs and poor text justification. These problems make the flow of text appear confusing to the reader and may even tend to change their reading preference.

Production of great and readable content should be your number one priority, make sure that your readers do not have a hard time when reading the book. You can use the .doc; .docx, or .html, formats, as they are the best to use because they can be changed to achieve the results you need.

Use the Simplified Formatting Guide to learn some tips on how you can easily format your book properly with no errors at all. One format error is recurred to all the pages in the document; make sure that the formatting of each page is precise.

### Duplicated Text

This is a problem that occurs as a result of having text that is repeated more than once while it is not supposed to be. This is mainly caused by use of copy-paste action, which may lead to you pasting information more than once.

Duplicated text includes mislabeled chapters, repeated chapter and at times phrases that are repeated several times in the same chapter or paragraph.

## Links

The links in your book should be able to guide your readers to the exact page where the information that they are looking for is. You can use your kindle device to first ensure that the links navigate straight to that intended page before you make the books available to the readers. If you are not in possession of a Kindle device you can use the Kindle Previewer to see how the content appears on a device.

Broken links are usually as a result of mistakes made in the link's URL or when you paste in the wrong location. Some of other linking problems that you can face include the following:

I.   Guide items that do not work properly –this is an item found on the "Go To" menu and it is used for navigating locations.
II.  Some links found on the Table of Content tend to not work.
III. A footnote that is unlinked.
IV.  External links that are prohibited
V.   Make sure that nothing is missing that is meant to guide the reader to some other page that will help them understand specific parts of the book better.

## Table Errors

When you use the tables to format data that is non-tabular you will cause some problems such as the table appearing half on the page. It is wise to avoid formatting text using tables or trying to make elements of the book appear in a certain way.

You should ensure that each table is visible at size 3, which is the default font size; otherwise it will be difficult for the larger audience to access your work.

Ensure that your tables do not consist of any non-tabular data and that when a reader is viewing them he or she does not need to pan them in any direction. Tables that force readers to take extra steps in order to view information that should be readily available are not much appreciated. If the data that you want to give must be in tabular form, trying breaking up the table into more cells and having more break points. When you use the Kindle Previewer and Kindle for PC, you do not always get the best preview of what the reader will view, it is wise that you use a Kindle device to see the final copy of your work.

## Missing Content

This is a problem that occurs when important parts of the book are left out: or even having references to some non-existent parts of the book. This is a major problem as missing information can lead to trouble and the readers may not even get the point clearly. For example, if you ask the readers to see a video for clear understanding of a concept and forget to link the video or if the video doesn't work, then the readers will have the information missing. This problem is major and can ruin the purpose of a book. Plus, incomplete sentences also fall in this category.

## Image formatting tip

When you are uploading an image you should ensure that it is in the .JPEG format and aligned to the center. Go to the top of the word screen and click "insert", and then choose the "picture" option, which will give you the option to choose the image that you want to use.

## Wrong Content

If your book has what is referred to as wrong content, it is not sold by Kindle, and they remove it very fast. This is when the client sells the reader the wrong book. This mainly happens when the writer uploads wrong information, uses the copy/paste function and messes with the information or when you make some updates to the book that are not correct. You can always avoid or solve this problem by always uploading the latest and clear version of the correct file.

## Kindle Unsuited Content

Some books such as puzzles, pattern, coloring and blank journals are not suitable for sale on Kindle and if you upload any, they will be brought down. Even those facing page translation books are not entertained (books with two sides, one with the translation of the language on the other.)

## Content That Disappoints

Some of the types of content that Kindle refers to as disappointing include the following;

- Content that you are marketing as a subscription that is used to redirect the readers to some other external buying site.
- Information that is available for free on the web is not for sale on Kindle unless you own the copyright of the content found on the web.
- Uploading information that can be used to solicit or advertise is not allowed.
- Use of content that is too short or that which looks so familiar to others that have been uploaded to Kindle before.
- When you are translating make sure that the information you come up with is of good quality.

Note: Plagiarism in any case is not tolerated.

# CHAPTER 6: MARKETING

When it comes to marketing your book, remember that quality is the cornerstone of good marketing. If you are looking at selling many books, find ways to create excitement in the consumers and make them want to read your book. The more interesting your book is the higher the chances of you selling many copies of it. The eBook should be so great that a customer, who was shopping for another book, sees it and gets interested in having a cop.

To ensure that your book is selling itself without any hiccups, you can use the following tips. They will guide you on how you can easily ensure that your book sells dozens of copies in no time.

**I.** A Persuasive Cover

The cover image that you use should be one that is flexible; this means an image that appears clear and in high quality when used in full size and even as a thumbnail. Amazons shows the cover images of your books as thumbnails in their automated merchandising, detail pages and even in search results. You can use the design service to come up with an awesome cover image. The cover should read the title properly and the image selected should be linked to the topic. Plus, you can use subtitles here to add curiosity and interest. Everything from font selection to color pattern is of importance here,

**II.** Compelling Book Description

When a reader is deciding on what book to buy or even lend from the Kindle Library they will first read the description of the book. The description explains what the whole book talks about and how to go about it. For example, if it a book about diabetes and its precautions then the description should highlight that the book covers ways to prevent or control diabetes. The description should be short and crisp. it is not the 'summary' of the book but more of an introduction that needs to leave an impact.

**III.** Proper Editing and Proofreading

When you are writing your book, it is obvious that you want some positive customer reviews so that you can sell the book. Avoid having typos and any form of grammatical errors in your book for readers give negative reviews on such books.

**IV.** Proper Author Profile

It is wise that you introduce yourself to your readers so that they feel like they know you already; this fosters a feeling of trust. The author profile is easy to complete, it includes a small biography, a bibliography, and a photo of yourself. You can also create a blog to speak with your readers to ensure that you are still relevant to them while you are in the process of coming up with the next best seller.

**V.** Promotion Using Kindle Countdown Deals

This is a form of promotion in which the early bird catches the worm. The countdown deals starts selling the book at a super cheap price for the first few readers to buy it and increases the price as time goes by. The eBook goes through several discounted lists before it makes it to the final selling price. The earlier you log in to the store, the cheaper you will buy the book for. This is a way of ensuring that you make sales while still getting reviews before your book starts to sell at the intended price.

**VI.** Create Print-on-demand Books

There are people who do not feel like they are actually reading unless they feel the texture of the book pages. In the spirit of availing your book both in digital and physical formats, Amazon.com provides a tool known as CreateSpace that can be used by readers to print out copies that they pay for. With the CreateSpace print-on-demand tool you will always have books to supply your readers without worrying about the printing or shipping fees.

**VII.** Online Book Promotion

Nowadays you can promote your book for free in the large array of social networks that we have. You should use networks that your readers are fond of visiting and promote your book there. There is also the choice of joining some online communities of like-minded people and promoting the book there or you can even use your blog or create a website for your book to boost its exposure and increase the sales. It is important that books are promoted on relevant websites, for example if it is a book about health then it should be promoted on health pages.

**VIII.** Uploading of Book Teasers

A teaser gets you in the mood and tells you what to to expect in the book. It also creates a craving for he book since you only share little details and try to get the attention of your readers. You then invite them to visit the Kindle Store and purchase the rest of the book there. Amazon has a place you can upload you trailers to on the Author Pages.

**IX.** Join the Amazon Associates Program

This program helps you create some special links to your book and make it look more professional. You can also create some widgets for interaction between readers and yourself. Whenever someone buys your book as a result of clicking on these links you will be earning an extra four percent.

Amazon.com offers tools that will help you self publish your book. The store also gives you a great customer base even when you are just a new writer on the rise.

# Chapter 7: Uploading Your Book to Amazon KDP

Uploading your book on Amazon KDP Select is not a very complicated or even hard process. It just needs you to be super attentive so that you do not do anything wrong for that will make you have to repeat the whole process.

Once you are through with writing your eBook and you are ready to take the next move towards publishing and selling it. There are some steps that you can follow to properly upload your book. After all the marketing you have done, it is time to quench the customer's thirst of waiting for your book, follow these step to upload it:

1.  **Step One**
    First sign in to Amazon KDP with you Amazon.com account or you can just open a new account.

2.  **Step Two**
    After you have logged in go and add a new title to your KDP Bookshelf to create a new publication –the book you are uploading.

3.  **Step Three**
    Now go and fill in all the necessary details of your book, this includes:
    - The name of the book.
    - Volume and Edition numbers
    - eBook description
    - The date details and language of the book
    - Publisher of ISBN
    - Copyright

4.  **Step Four**
    The next step is to upload your eBook to Amazon KDP Bookshelf. Use a format such as Web Page, *HTM and *HTML. When you upload your book successfully, you will be given an option to view how the book will appear when published. If you are satisfied with the work that you have done and how it appears, save the file.

5.  **Step Five**
    You will then be taken to a page on which you are supposed to choose the price of your eBook. You are also to choose the type of royalty that you would like, there

are two (35% for books going for a price ranging between $2.99 and $9.99 and 70% for those going for a price between $2.99 and $200) royalty options. The price range depends on several requirements as well, such as the size of the file.

**6.** Step Six

Now you are done with all that is required on your book, wait for about twenty-four hours for Amazon to officially approve your book.

Follow the steps as they are provided to ensure that you do not have to keep repeating the process.

# Chapter 8: Understanding The KDP Select Global Fund Amount

In this chapter you will be learning more about the Kindle Direct Publishing Select Global Fund and how it is calculated among other things.

## Your Share of the KDP Select of the Fund

The calculations of your share of the royalties are based on how much your book is read for. It also is inclusive of the times that your book is downloaded by the customers of kindle Owners' Lending Library. The numbers of times that your book was read is compared to the times that all the KDP Select titles were viewed.

The amount of money that you will get each month will depend on the number of times that your books were read and the total number of titles viewed, this means that the increase in the number of titles does affect your share positively or negatively depending on the numbers viewed. Since the pay starts to come in when your book gets more than ten percent viewed, this creates some form of compelling among authors and publishers to do better.

When you are a citizen of another country other than the US you will still receive the money in USD but the KDP Select Global Fund Select staff can convert the currency for you of informational purposes.

The amount of money in the Kindle Direct Publishing Select Global Fund is usually announced on the KDP website and the Community Pages for the sake of transparency. When you are open about what you are doing, people will ted to trust you and in case of the Kindle store, it means that they will get more and more writers, this reflects into profits in the near future.

When you upload and publish your eBook with Kindle Direct Publishing Select, it is given an Amazon Prime badge that will identify it when readers are searching for books in that niche. The badge makes it available when customers or people who want to lend it in Kindle Owners' Lending Library are searching it.

If your book available in the Kindle Owners' Lending Library it can be read by the customers as many times as they like but only once per month. You only qualify for royalty when a Prime customer downloads your book for the first time. Although the customer can never pay for that same book again after that time. You can also earn royalties if you read your own book if you happen to be eligible to use the Kindle Owners' Lending Library.

The Lending for Kindle is an application or tool in which you can be able to lend a book that you have already bought to your friends and family. Unlike in Kindle Owners' Lending Library where you have to be from certain countries, the Lending for Kindle works for anyone anywhere in the world.

The reader's can only to access the books in the Kindle Owners' Lending Library through a Kindle device, the use of Kindle application cannot work on these kind of books. When you decide not to renew the enrollment of your book in the library, the customers can keep it till it is returned and you will still be able to earn some royalty when a unique KOLL customer purchases and downloads an eBook.

You can make all your books easier to find by putting them in the Kindle Unlimited, a subscription service currently only available to customers in the US, the UK, Brazil, Spain, France, Canada, Germany and Italy. With the use of this subscription service, the readers can read your books as many times as they want for a whole month. They only get to continue accessing the books the next month if they pay the fee.

Once you enroll your book in KDP Select it automatically gets enrolled into the Kindle Unlimited and Kindle Owners' Lending Library. For you to qualify for Kindle Unlimited you have to meet the requirements set for KDP Select and enroll your book there. When you enroll to these services, the price of your book should remain constant for at least one month.

# CHAPTER 9: PASSIVE INCOME GENERATION

The eBook publishing business on Amazon.com and KDP Select is one that can become a major income generating business for you if you do everything right and follow the instructions and guidelines provided in this book.

A passive income is very easy when you decide to work on eBooks and sell them on platforms such Amazon.com.

## Your Investment

You will only need to invest in time and a few dollars to get your first eBook off the ground. Plan how and when you will be writing the book and an estimation of the time that it will take you to complete drafting the whole book.

After you have finished writing the whole draft and revised it to come up with a good eBook, it is time to move to the next step. Design an e-cover for your eBook to make it look great and attractive to your customers. If you do not have any knowledge of designing you can outsource and have your e-cover designed for a pretty fair price.

The investment of the whole project will cost you nothing much other than the time you spent writing and the few dollars that you used to pay for the high quality e-cover.

It is possible to scale this business by hiring writers to write your books for you. In doing this one is able to leverage their time and focus on creating covers, promoting their books and getting reviews. Another way to leverage oneself is to hire Virtual Assistants who can do a lot of the grunt work for you. A virtual assistant can come in extremely handy for help in research and marketing.

A book generates passive income once you put it up for sale; it will be making you money even when you are fast asleep. This is one way of earning extra income on the side without having to mess with your daily routine.

This is a way that is making people six figures incomes in less than a year. Work hard and ensure that your eBooks do not have even the slightest mistakes and once the readers notice the quality of your work, you will be well on your way to a better income that generates itself as you are doing other activities or even writing more eBooks in order to make even more cash. The beginning is difficult but if you think you can do it then you surely can.

# CONCLUSION

Thank you again for downloading this book!

It is my genuine and sincere hope that this book will help you out in coming up with the bestselling books on Amazon Kindle Direct Publish Select. The focus of this book is to help you understand exactly how Amazon Self Publishing makes you money.

You will come across some obstacles in your writing but do not despair and remember that you can achieve all that you put your mind to. Use the tricks in writing so as to come up with a great book that has no grammatical errors, no plagiarism or duplication in this case and any images used in your book should be of the highest quality to prevent them from giving you headaches once you are done.

Now that you have this knowledge you can always come up with great eBooks and ensure that they are in the perfect format. You have also gained knowledge on how to market and promote your book using the Internet, social networks and blogs. Keep going through the information and in time you will not need to go back to this book to look for some solution because you will already have it in your head. But also be aware that all these online businesses are evolving super fast so if you have any hopes of staying relevant in this field you should always be informed on what is the next new and hip way of making your books attractive to the new requirements of the audience.

To hear about Entrepreneur Publishing's new books first (and to be notified when there are free promotions), sign up to their New Release Mailing List.

Finally, if you enjoyed this book, please take the time to share your thoughts and post a review on Amazon. It'd be greatly appreciated!

Thank you and good luck!

# Preview Of '<u>Content Marketing Strategies: How Delivering Sensational Value Can Help You Build A Digital Media Empire</u>'

## WHAT IS THE VALUE OF SUCCESSFUL CONTENT ON YOUR WEBSITE?

Basically, the Internet was created as a source of information. Thus, if you own a website, it must provide relevant and important contents for your audience. If the content on your website doesn't provide the information that your users want, then it will be of little value to your site visitors who surf the Internet.

Are you someone who always post a new blog or article on your website just to add something new and fresh, and then wonder why you miss out new readers and web traffic?

Well you have to keep in mind that people are visiting blogs and websites because they're looking for information. They often require solutions or answers to their problems, wants, needs and desires. If you want to gain new readers and have your existing ones return again and again, then provide them something relevant and valuable.

### WHY IS CONTENT THE MOST IMPORTANT ASPECT OF YOUR WEBSITE?

Websites are valuable platforms to communicate effectively whatever message you want to get across your audience. If you want to achieve success in any of your online endeavor, you have to answer the questions of your visitors or satisfy their need for information and knowledge.

In order to achieve this, you will need a website that is rich with useful content. The content of your website must be up to date, well organized, relevant and written uniquely on every page of the website. Your web content must also be written as if you're talking to your audience.

## How To Make Your Content Useful and Informative

In order to write informative and valuable posts, you need first to know the issues your audience are dealing with, the problems they are facing, the questions they are asking, their needs, wants and desires. After identifying these things, it is the time for you to research and determine your niche.

To do this, you can find some of the most popular websites within your niche. Such sites can provide you with some valuable insight about your potential customers. This will also help you determine their age group, location, income level and even their gender.

You can now write based on the data gathered. Of course, you're not going to write in similar manner for a group of young adult males as you would for senior males. Your choice of language, general advice and tone must be according to the information obtained.

If you want to know the problems your readers face, visit some forums. Note their questions, and write a post or an article to answer them.

**Some of the things you need to do are:**

1. Write tutorials, tips and unique articles that will draw the attention and get the interest of your visitors and get them to return to your website.

2. Always update your content to keep the website interesting and fresh. If you want to have good traffic, keep in mind that major Search Engines always look for websites that offer useful information.

3. Avoid the use of jargon when writing web content. Use only familiar words.

4. Make your content Search Engine friendly by making a content rich site that contains texts instead of images.

5. Consider your website design. It must attract both the Search Engines and visitors.

Indeed, content marketing is one of the best marketing approaches you should use to obtain your online endeavors and reach an increased number of clients. Whether you have an online business or a personal blog, having a content-rich website is important to achieve online success.

Click here to check out the rest of Content Marketing Strategies: How Delivering Sensational Value Can Help You Build A Digital Media Empire on Amazon.

Or go to: http://amzn.to/1a8dfYp

# MORE BOOKS FOR ENTREPRENEURS

Click here to check out the rest of Entrepreneur Publishing's books on Amazon.

Below you'll find some of my other popular books that are popular on Amazon and Kindle as well. Simply click on the links below to check them out. Alternatively, you can visit my author page on Amazon to see other work done by me.

How Audiobooks Make You Smarter: 7 Little Known Ways Audio Books Can Boost Memory Capacity And Increase Intelligence

How To Write A Book And Publish On Amazon: Make Money With Amazon Kindle, CreateSpace And Audiobooks

Gardening For Entrepreneurs: Gardening Techniques For High Yield, High Profit Crops

Speed Reading For Entrepreneurs: Seven Speed Reading Tactics To Read Faster, Improve Memory And Increase Profits

Content Marketing Strategies: How Delivering Sensational Value Can Help You Build A Digital Media Empire

Video Marketing: How To Produce Viral Films And Leverage Facebook, YouTube, Instagram And Twitter To Build A Massive Audience

If the links do not work, for whatever reason, you can simply search for these titles on the Amazon website to find them.

www.ingramcontent.com/pod-product-compliance
Lightning Source LLC
Chambersburg PA
CBHW071018180526
45168CB00003B/1468